The Survivors Series

Corvettes For The Road

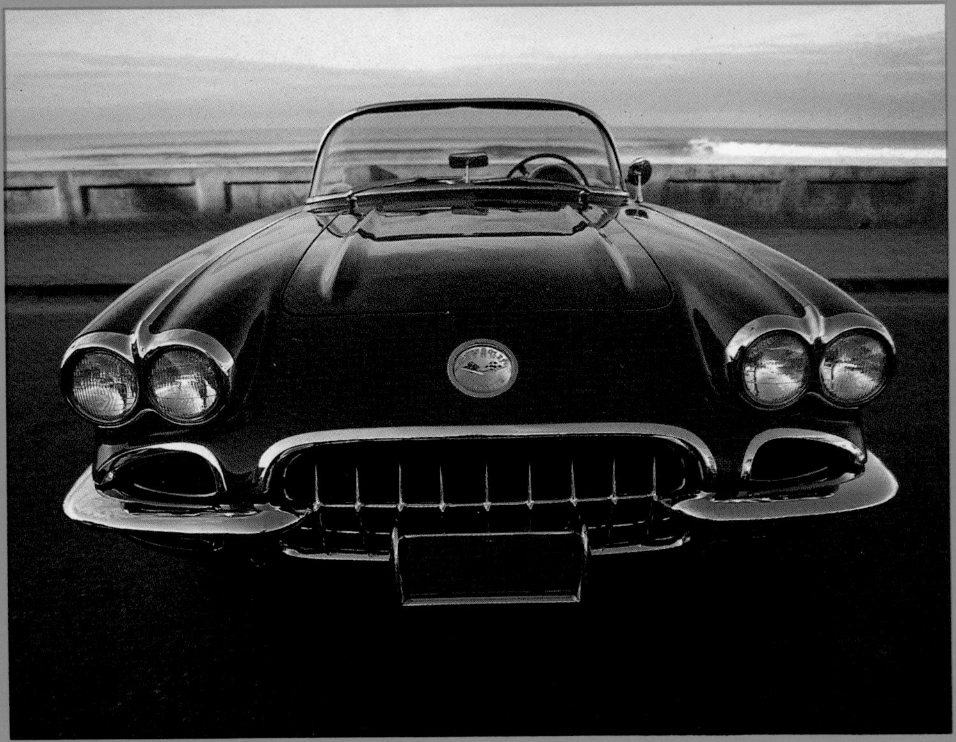

CORVETTES

Published by Motorbooks International
Publishers and Wholesalers, Inc.
Osceola, Wisconsin, U.S.A.
Copyright 1984 by Henry Rasmussen.
ISBN 0-87938-182-5.
Library of Congress number 84-11497
Printed in Hong Kong by
South China Printing Company.

FOR THE ROAD

Beginning of it all! General Motors' chief stylist, Harley Earl had the dream. Bob McLean put the shape on paper. Stylists even decided location of axles and engine. Then came engineering, by Maurice Olley, under Ed Cole, chief engineer.

Power source was a 235 cubic-inch, over head valve, straight six. Basically a prewar truck engine! But new manifolds, higher compression ratio (eight to one), plus other improvements, raised output to 150 bhp. Three sidedraft Carter carburetors were used. Zero to 60 took 11 seconds. The quarter mile took almost 18. Zero to 100 took 39. Top speed was 108 mph.

The frame was new. Front and rear suspension (rigid axle), brakes (11-inch drums) and steering were adapted stock Chevrolet components. The body was fiberglass—a first for a production car! Overall weight of the 167-inch long, 72-inch wide, 52-inch low car, was 2900 pounds. Price was $3250. Only 300 were made, all white roadsters with red interiors.

Although the Corvette concept was well accepted, Powerglide—a two-speed automatic—coupled with the lack of performance, dampened the enthusiasm. The Corvette was off to a slow start!

Classic of the second-generation Corvettes! Changed styling had come in 1956. No rear fins now. Conventional headlights. Sculptured side panels. Roll-up windows. Exterior door handles. Clean and mature lines. But in 1957, came the clincher, fuel injection! A first for an American car.

European-born engineer and race driver Zora Arkus-Duntov, who had come aboard in 1953, began to make his marque, gradually improving both performance and handling.

Underneath the new body, things were basically the same as before (except for Zora's subtle changes), as were overall weight and dimensions. Performance wise, Chevrolet's new small block V-8 made a difference. It was first used in 1955 models, 235 cubic-inch then; now 283. Four tuning stages were available. The strongest had 283 bhp. And fuel injection! And optional 4-speed! Compression was 10.5 to one. Zero to 60 took 5.8 seconds; the quarter mile, 14. Top speed was 133 mph.

After a slow start, the Corvette was off and running. Production was 6,339 (1,040 fuel-injected). Price was $3427, (higher with options). V-8 power with fuel injection saved the Corvette. Nothing could stop it now!

53

57

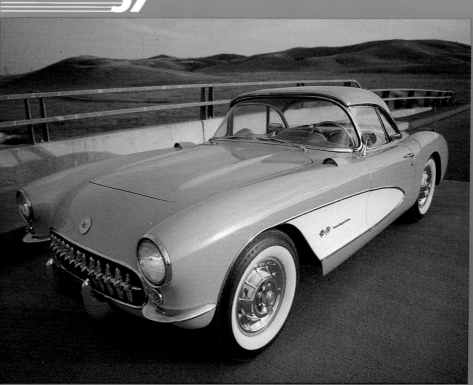

The styling race was on! In 1958 the Corvette grew nine inches longer and two inches wider (due to bulging grille and bumpers). It had been adorned with twin headlights and two extra grille openings, as well as more chrome and fake louvers. The louvers on the hood were all gone by 1960. So were the chromed bars on the trunk lid. For the better!

For 1960 Zora Arkus-Duntov reworked the suspension, improving both handling and ride comfort. For the first time, an anti-roll bar was fitted at the rear. The one at the front was up-sized. The steering now became closer to neutral.

If the styling-race was on, so was the horsepower race. For 1960, Duntov squeezed 315 bhp (most of four options) from the 283, mainly by increasing compression to 11 to one and enlarging the plenum chamber of the injection unit.

In spite of the increased use of aluminum over the years, weight of the 1960 was 3,100 pounds. Price was $3872. Incredibly, the Powerglide had survived, and was a $199 option. For comparison, the 4-speed manual was a $188 option.

For the first time, production topped ten thousand (10,261). The Corvette was really flying now!

Last year of the second-generation Corvettes! Styling had been modified in 1961, a result of Bill Mitchell having taken over as chief stylist. No teeth in the grille. New rear. For 1962 the cove in the side panel had no chrome molding. The cove was therefore always the color of the car.

The 1962 was last in many ways. Last with rigid rear axle. Last with optional power top. Last with exterior trunk opening. Last with exposed headlights.

Under the hood, the 1962 sported a bigger engine, a 327. It came in three performance options. Top of the trio was the 360 bhp version. In spite of the increase in power, performance was equal to that of the first fuel-injected 1957; the weight had crept up with another 150 pounds.

Sales skyrocketed! Total production, 14,531. Price, also up, was $4227, base. The Powerglide was still hanging on; price, unchanged. Four-speed, also unchanged. But things could not stay as they were, in spite of sales records. The Corvette had been around for almost a decade. It was time for a radical change. And, Duntov and Mitchell had a winner waiting!

60

62

Classic year of the third-generation Corvettes! Controversial then, the split-window coupe now stands out as the most representative of all Corvette designs. Mitchell and his team had created a bold, beautiful new look, available in both coupe and convertible. The new car was three inches lower, and slightly shorter, on four inches shorter wheelbase.

New exterior covered new interior, except engine and transmission and their various options, which were carry-overs. The frame was new, and, most notable, the Corvette now had independent rear suspension. Arkus-Duntov's efforts in engineering were just as succesful as Mitchell's in styling, producing a car with vastly improved ride and handling. Brakes were also improved, but were still drums. Power-assisted brakes and steering were available as an option for the first time.

Although weight was up, performance was unchanged, thanks to improved aerodynamics. Price was $4394, base. Production was up drastically, 21,513 units. The creators of the new Corvette had reason to be satisfied; they already knew how well their creation looked, and how well it performed, but now they knew the buying public also agreed.

The convertible Sting Ray was it! The convertible and the coupe had sold equally well in 1963. Now the convertible pulled ahead. Almost twice as many were sold. The trend began in 1964, when the split window was removed. Vision considerations had won out. The convertible was indeed very well-balanced, very clean-looking, very European-looking.

Most years have features that make them unique. The 1965 was the first with disc brakes. And the last with fuel injection! The discs were fitted all around, standard. But drums were still available. Opting for them saved $64!

In the engine compartment, there was a wide choice. No less than six tuning stages! The 250 bhp and 300 bhp used four-barrel Carters. The 350 and 365 featured Holleys. The 375 used fuel injection. All these took their power from the 327. Add to these the real brute! The 425 bhp option. This was the new 396 cubic-inch engine, fitted with a four-barrel Holley. A special hood bulge had to be created! Added to this could be another new option. Side-mounted exhaust pipes! It cost a mere $134 to attach this sure attention-getter.

Base price was $4106. Total number produced, 23,562.

63

65

Last of the third-generation Corvettes. The 1967 almost never happened, that is, the new Corvette was supposed to have come that year, but final testing revealed that the car was still not ready. So, the old style was carried on yet another year. In a sense it made the car better. The body was further cleaned up; certain trim and emblems were removed and the fender vents, functional since 1965, became five angled slots and the best looking yet.

In the engine compartment, things had also received attention; there was the basic 300 bhp engine, plus four options; the L71 was the 435 bhp 427, top of the line. Fuel injection was no longer used. Instead three two-barreled Holleys were employed. A hood bulge had been designed for that option. True, there was another option, the now famous L88. But with aluminum heads and a reported output of 560 bhp, it was really someting just for the racing minded.

Safety concerns had eliminated the knock-off wheel; the new bolt-on cover looked the same, but had a wingless cap covering the nuts. Base price was $4327. Total production was 22,940, down from the 1966 figure of 27,720.

Second year of the fourth generation! In 1968, the new car met with mixed reactions, due to lack of development.

The new Corvette took its inspiration from Mitchell's Mako Shark experimental cars. Stylists Larry Shinoda, David Holls and Henry Haga worked out the production look. It was two inches lower and seven inches longer than the first Sting Ray, but kept the same wheelbase. Width was about the same, but track a little wider. Rims were 7-inch; in 1969, 8-inch.

Under the new shell, things were basically the same as in 1967. Due to organizational changes at GM and a long illness, Duntov had not been all that involved with the new car. In 1969, he was back again, and his touch was again apparent; the Sting Ray badge reappeared, now spelled Stingray.

Engine options were spectacular: seven, in addition to the basic. The small block was reintroduced, now 350 cubic inches. The L71 option 427 had 435 bhp. But its zero to 60 time did not creep below six seconds; the new body was heavier.

Price was $4400. Production numbers show that the trend had turned in favor of the coupe, 22,154 compared to 16,608, for a total of 38,762. A new record!

67

69

After seven years, it was really time for a new design. But the 1975 Corvette still looked the same. Of course, the climate was not all that healthy in the marketplace. Not for sports cars! Smog rules. Safety laws. World wide depression.

The 1975 lacked many of the features that had made the Corvette! There was no Mark IV engine. No genuine dual exhaust. And it was the last year of the convertible!

Adding to all the other negatives, 1975 was the first year for the catalytic converter; unleaded fuel had to be used. The front and rear by now sported impact-resistant designs that added weight, now up to 3,660 pounds.

On the engine front, the decline of the Corvette as a purist car showed clearly. There was only one option, a 205 bhp, 350 cubic-inch small block. The base version developed 165 bhp. Zero to 60 took almost 10 seconds. The quarter mile, almost 17. Not much better than 20 years earlier!

The price did not decline, however. Base was $6810; more with necessary options. Total production was 38,465. Convertibles accounted for 4,629 of that total.

Year of the Silver Anniversary! Year of the Pace Car! Both exterior and interior had received a facelift. The rear had become a fastback, with a large window. Instruments and armrests had been redesigned and the fastback style allowed for a somewhat larger luggage space.

The Corvette performed the honors of pace car at the 1978 Indianapolis 500. Thus the limited edition. According to initial plans there would only be one thousand units made. In the end, 6,502 were assembled, approximately one car for every Corvette dealer in the country. The Pace Car featured prominent front and rear spoilers, and two-tone paint; black on the upper half of the body, and silver on the bottom half. There were also special decals included with the Pace Car, but most owners let them stay in their wrappers.

There was still not much to brag about under the hood. Still only one option, now producing 220 bhp—15 horses more. The base price was $9351. Base price for the Pace Car was $13,653; that still did not include the stronger engine. It was another $525. Demand was so great that many a Pace Car went for upwards of $20,000. Total production, 46,776.

The old body style was still hanging on. By now it had been drastically updated. For 1980 there were new front and rear bumper assemblies. Front and rear spoilers were built into these. Those spoilers definitely improved the aerodynamics. And looks!? It had become quite "awesome", to use a word popularized by another manufacturer.

In the engine compartment things looked only a little brighter than before. There were two performance levels, but not in California, where tight emission restrictions caused GM to offer only the 305 cubic-inch, 180 bhp unit, while elsewhere L82 was the most powerful option, giving 230 bhp. The fact that GM engineers had managed to lighten the car by 250 pounds, was commendable, but did not improve performance to the level of the good old days.

If things looked bleak on the performance front, they looked much brighter in the area of creature comfort; there were no less than seven options that had to do with sound equipment. Stereo with CB and power antenna cost $391 (same as removable roof panels of glass). Base price was $13,140. The total number of cars produced was 40,614.

The old Corvette had been around for fifteen seasons. There had been many experimentals. And much talk. But with the old selling so well, wishes of stylists and engineers did not count. But, finally, in 1983 there was a new Corvette!

The new frame and suspension got highest marks. Responsible was Dave McLellan. He had worked with Duntov before taking charge, starting with the 1976 model. The styling was clean and beautiful, on a par with the best from Europe, but still unmistakably Corvette. Responsible was Jerry Palmer, working under Charles Jordan and Irv Rybicki.

Length was down nine inches, to 176.5. Width was up two inches, to 71. Height was down over an inch, to 46.7. Wheelbase was shortened to 96.2. Weight was down over three hundred pounds, to 3,200. The engine was about the only carry-over. The 350 cubic-inch put out 205 bhp. Zero to 60 took just over 7 seconds. Top speed was 140 mph.

Price was $24,600. A drastic jump. But it was very much car for the money! There are no 1983's. All are 1984's. Total units produced, to the end of March, is 37,389. The present assembly line pace works out to three thousand a month.

80

84

The Beauty of the Beast...

Few sports cars, if any, have had as much printed about them as has the Corvette. There are uncountable articles, numerous specialty magazines, a variety of club publications, and scores of books... In spite of this abundance, there always seems to be room for more; there always seems to be talk of that final, definitive book... Well, this is not the one!

In fact, none of the books in The Survivors Series claim to give a comprehensive documentation of the technical and historical aspects of a marque in question. The emphasis of The Survivors Series has always been on the beauty of the cars...

In this new volume, ninth in the series, this emphasis is even more obvious. For two reasons. First, the Corvette is a photographer's dream, so incredibly flamboyant... I simply couldn't resist being carried away by its appearence! Second, as a favor, General Motors Design allowed special access to their long-stored-away photographic files, making it possible to document the styling aspect of the creation process as seldom before.

So, don't look for information on the location of serial numbers, or complete listings of options, or explanations of fuel-injection systems... Instead, lean back in your favorite chair and open the pages to the beauty of the Corvette, seen from a variety of perspectives. For a Corvette is much more than just suspension geometry, gear ratios, and gas mileage... A Corvette also deserves to be looked at, driven, remembered... That's the beauty of it...The beauty of the beast!

Somewhat pretentious, the emblem of the first Corvette carried an aura of racing distinction; there was no involvement in racing until the introduction of the second-generation Corvette. But from then on it more than made up for the initial innocence; over the years Corvettes were perennial class winners at Sebring and captured a long string of regional and national SCCA championships. Best of all, its eminent career is far from over yet!

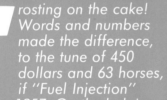 rosting on the cake! Words and numbers made the difference, to the tune of 450 dollars and 63 horses, if "Fuel Injection" adorned the cove of a 1957. On the bulging hood of a 1967, the "427" could mean a difference of 437 dollars and 135 horses. The "Limited Edition" decal on the side panel of a 1978, meant 4302 dollars, but it did not buy any extra horses!

Single is all right, but double is better! That seemed to be the reasoning among automotive stylists in the mid-fifties. Naturally, the Corvette received its share too. The single light was last seen on the 1957, its simple "sugar scoop" rear unit pictured on the opposite page. From 1958 on, Corvettes were stuck with the double lights. The double rear lights became something of a trademark, carried on to the 1984.

Wheels of fortune! Pictured on this page, the 53-55 wheel cover (right), and the 56-62 (far right and above). Shown on the opposite page, the 63-66 optional alloy wheel (top left), the 68 and on standard wheel cover (top right), the 76 and on optional aluminum wheel (bottom left), and the new 84 wheel (bottom right).

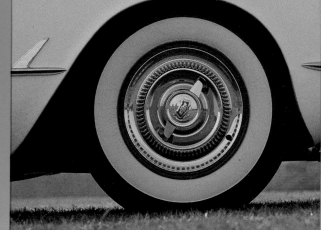

Dash design remained the same after the new body came in 1956. Shown above, the 1953 interior, the 1957 to the right. Restyled dash was introduced in 1958. It stayed until 1963. A 1960 is pictured on the opposite page (far right). Shown below it, the controversial Sting Ray dash as it appears on a 1965 roadster. In 1968 it was again time for a restyling. A 1969, minus roof panels, is pictured in the middle.

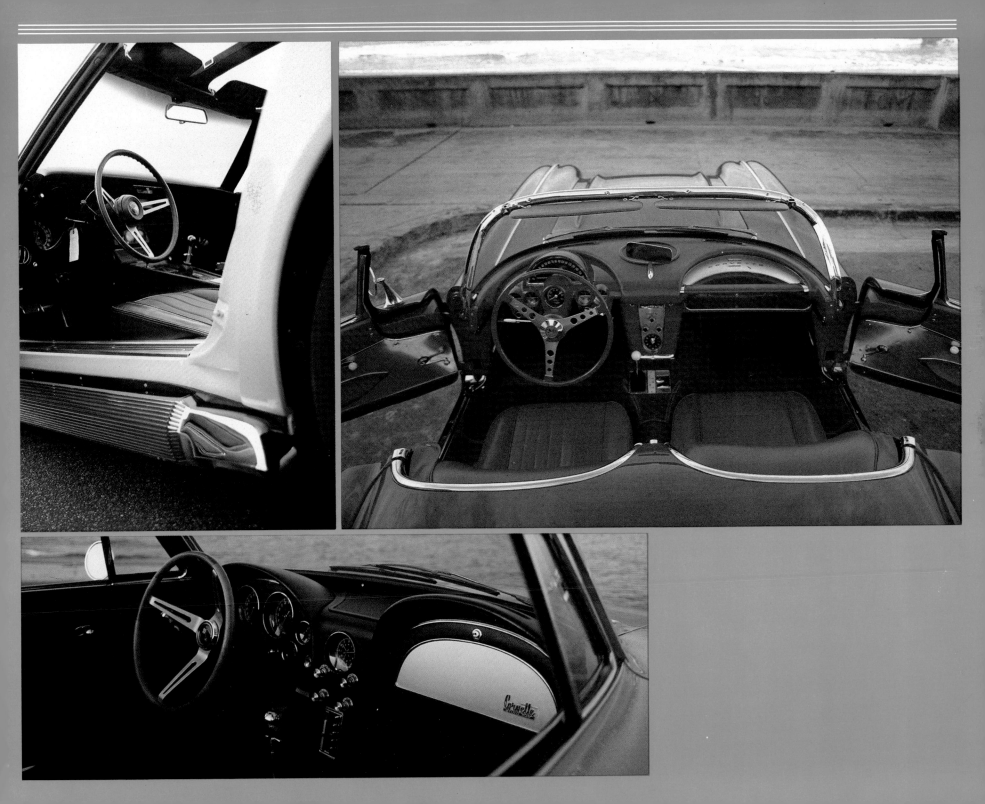

Overembellished? Sure! But the dashes, instruments, steering wheels of these early cars represent an era when the possibilities seemed endless, in the field of styling, as well as in more profound matters. The driver's view in a 1953 is seen to the left. The odometer, by the way, has just rolled over to the nine-thousand-mile figure. To the right, the impressive view in a 1960. And above, the same basic style seen in a 1962. These second-generation steering wheels are by far the best looking of the lot.

Shown in this spread, engines that highlight a spectacular rise to power! On this page (top), the straight six of 1953, with its three Carter carburetors and 150 bhp. On the opposite page (far left), the 283 bhp of 1957, a V-8, fuel injected for the first time. Next, the 360 bhp of 1963, still fuel injected. The 1967 435 bhp (near left) had given up fuel injection for the triple Holleys. The peak of performance, the 1969 ZL-1 (above), with its aluminum block, unofficially producing 580 bhp!

A reoccuring theme in fifties styling was a design element that became prominently exemplified in McDonald's "golden arches". In Corvette styling this element can be found, for example, on the side panel of a 1957 (left), or on the door panel of a 1960 (upper right). Soft curves could be found all over, in the wheel cover of a 1962 (above), or in the lower edge of the dash on a 1953 (right). Note that the large dial, the tachometer, has an unusual feature, a revolution accumulator.

Backgrounds can say much about a car. To the left, the most power packed of all Corvettes for the road, the 1969 ZL-1, is mated with the ultimate performance machine, the locomotive. To the right, the larger-than-life plumbing of a waste-recycling plant (no double meaning intended) reinforces the resourceful lines of the 1978 Pace Car. Above, the slick surface of a tile wall emphasizes the clean and purposeful design of the 1984 Corvette.

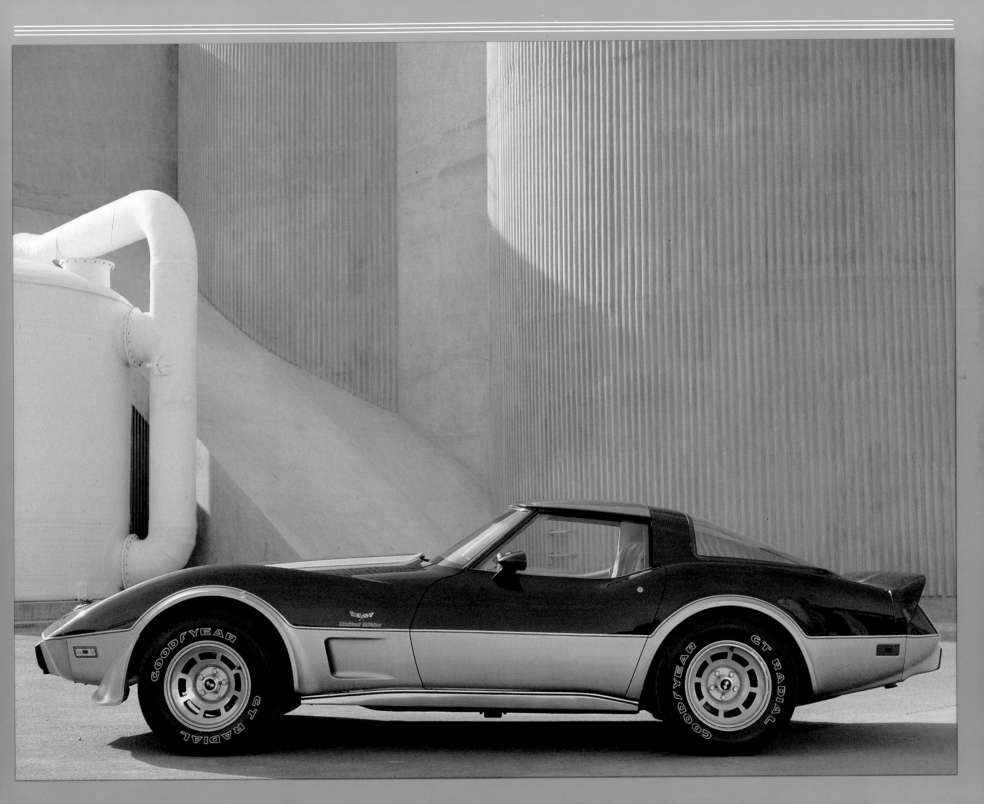

On historic ground! Corvette designer Jerry Palmer poses with the finished product. A team effort, to be sure, it is still an experience afforded few men, to drive a car that is so much the product of his own creative efforts. The photos were taken in the closed viewing area at General Motors Technical Center, where all Corvettes, except the 1953, have first been shown to corporate dignitaries.

A Homecoming of Sorts.

Nineteen fifty-three was a year of beginnings as well as endings. It was a significant year. But maybe every year seems that way when you look back and discover that history has already been made. Stalin died. That was the end of something. The fighting in Korea also came to an end. And Truman gave way for Eisenhower. Another ending. Another beginning.

But some things didn't change. In boxing, Rocky Marciano held on to his heavyweight crown. And in baseball, the Yankees won the World Series for the fifth time in a row.

In the movies there's always something new. The craze that year was 3-D. Anyone remember seeing *Kiss Me Kate* through those cardboard-frame glasses?

On the automotive front, the wraparound windshield made its production car debut. And General Motors introduced a new sports car, the Corvette. That, certainly, turned out to be the beginning of something!

I have just finished shooting Corvette number 181. It sits parked on the green grass of a football field. Right on top of the fifty-yard line. Tooth-grinned and spaceship-tailed, it sits there as a symbol of things past.

The round sloping front fenders with their faired-in headlights might have been inspired by the 356 Porsche, first seen in 1949. Jaguar's XK 120 also came in 1949, but there's nothing about the looks of the Corvette that resembles the Jaguar. Unless the headlights, meant to have ple-

(continued on overleaf)

The first public viewing of a Corvette took place at the Motorama in New York on January 17, 1953. The event was held in the Grand Ballroom of the Waldorf-Astoria. Pictured to the left, Number One surrounded by an admiring crowd. Notice that the spear on the side panel has its fin pointing down; on the production model it was changed to point up. On this page, two dream cars for the 1954 Motorama. Above, the fastback Corvair (all Chevrolet models had to begin with a "C" in those days). Right, a Corvette with a removable hardtop. The hardtop became an option in 1956. The Corvair never made it to production.

O f the three hundred Corvettes created in 1953, one fourth are still missing. The discovery of a lost one sends ripples of excitement through the Corvette fraternity. Especially when it has as little as nine thousand original miles on the odometer, and still rolls on its original set of tires!

Chip Miller, of York, Pennsylvania, owns this Survivor, chassis number E53F001181. The first owner drove it on vacation to Colorado, but didn't like it, so he sent it home on the train. Sentenced to life in an unheated garage, it did not emerge until 1972.

xiglass covers, were influenced by the C-type, Jaguar's 1951 Le Mans winner. The grille looks somewhat like that of the 1952 Mercedes 300 SL. But the Mercedes didn't arrive until after the shape of the Corvette was already set. Maybe that grille could be traced back to Pinin Farina's 1947 Cisitalia? Be that as it may, the Corvette still is an original. An American original.

It's homecoming week. And time for the game to begin. Players come running in on the field. All of them too young to remember. But they're curious. Even in the midst of their excitement they must stop to admire the object that tells the story of another time, happily simple, optimistically limitless, innocently wild.

The referees are old enough to remember. But they tell us to move the car. Now!

I'm behind the wheel. What a wheel! Big. Beautiful. I'm sitting close to it with my arms doubled-up. The feel is that of an old car. But the sensation that stands out comes from the Power-glide, that smooth, even motion, accompanied by that smooth, even exhaust note. Nothing sporty about that sound! The Powerglide makes the straight-six sound like a boat. Not a speed boat. Just a plain old motor boat.

The odometer turns over to 9061. I feel nervous about putting miles on it. The owner, Chip Miller, one of the most knowledgeable, genuine, and amicable Corvette enthusiasts you'll ever meet, and partner in The Flea Marketeers (which organizes the big twice-annual swap-meet events in Carlisle, Pennsylvania,) sits in the passenger seat. As we roll slowly down the main street of York (the top is down), I stay aware of the surrounding traffic like never before; this car isn't only worth a lot of money, it's also a piece of history. It can't be replaced!

"One of my friends heard the car was for sale. They all knew I was crazy about Corvettes, so he told me. The owner of a radio station in Niagara Falls had bought it new. It came out of the estate after his death and was never advertised. Those early cars were only sold to celebrities, so I guess owning a radio station must have qualified him. He didn't drive it much. But he did take it twice all

There is a curious case of missing files in the archives at GM Design. The reference catalog shows subjects and numbers. But all early negatives pertaining to the Corvette are missing from its cabinet—destroyed, lost, stolen—who knows? The picture above, the only in the file, dated November 29, 1952, shows the prototype top mechanism just a month and a half before introduction. It may be the earliest photograph still in existence. Left and right, dated August 26, 1953, the Motorama car in the lobby of the GM Building. Above, right, dash of the production version.

the way to Colorado. The second time he must have become fed up with the primitive weather protection or something, because he shipped it back on the train and put it away in his garage. When I got the car in 1972 it had 8,788 miles and a 1962 sticker.

"I went to see the car. It was sitting by itself in a small garage. It was terribly filthy. I could hardly tell it was white. I wiped off an area on the fender and saw that the paint was fine, but very yellow. The top was up. I checked it, too. It was like new under the dirt. Not a stitch was torn. And I checked the serial number to be sure it was a 1953. At first I could hardly believe the low mileage. But the more dirt I wiped off the more I saw of the condition of the car, and I began to think it was possible. I also looked at that engine revolution counter on the tach. It checked out. The mileage was original!

"I gave them my bid. It was high. It was high, back in 1972! It doesn't sound like much today. But I wanted that car badly!

"Every time the phone rang I was a nervous wreck! For a long time, long for me, I didn't hear from them, so I finally called. A policeman had offered 2500 dollars. But that wasn't anywhere close to my bid. So the car was mine!

"I can remember it was in the middle of the winter. And it had been snowing. And I had an open trailer. The car did run, although a muffler was shot and the fuel pump was leaking, but I didn't want to put any miles on it, so I trailered it in spite of the bad weather.

"It took me a couple of months to clean it up. I used soap and water. It hasn't been restored, except for some minor details. But that's the way I want it. Let others discuss what an original 53 should look like. Mine is still the way it was when it came from the factory!

"How about the radio?" I ask. We're out on the open road now. The boat is plowing through the fresh autumn air, that monotonous exhaust note coming smooth and even.

"Original, too!" Chip says. "In fact, if you push this button, it will play *How Much Is That Doggie in the Window?*"!

Rock 'n' Roll Rocket.

It's 1957. Khrushchev consolidates his power in Moscow. Castro marches on Havana. And Great Britain becomes the third nation to explode a hydrogen bomb. At home, Eisenhower wins another term. Communist-hunter McCarthy dies in May. And there are race riots in Little Rock.

In sports, Floyd Patterson is boxing's new heavyweight champion. And the Milwaukee Braves beat the New York Yankees for the World Series title.

At the movies, Doris Day and Rock Hudson are the big box-office attractions. The Oscar goes to *The Bridge on the River Kwai*.

Radios and juke boxes across the nation glow red hot with Pat Boone's *Love Letters in the Sand* and Elvis Presley's *Jailhouse Rock*.

And in October, Moscow's Sputnik, the first earth satellite, awakens Americans to the dawn of the space age.

Somewhat enigmatically, with the arrival of a new age, the new Corvette had lost its rocket ship taillights. But then, they were always more of a Buck Rogers fantasy than a Wernher von Braun reality.

The new Corvette style had come in 1956. From the front, the grille was unchanged, but the headlights were now conventional, set high in the more drawn-out fender pontoons.

On the hood, two parallel bulges, like on the Mercedes 300SL, had been added. The new headlight arrangement could also be traced to the 300SL. (Photographs taken in early 1955

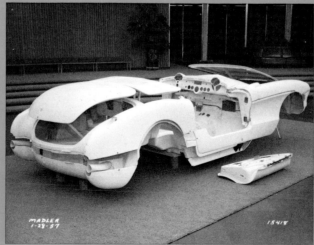

At least two full-size models showing the suggested restyling for 1956 were posed for viewing and photography on February 1, 1955. The sequence on the opposite page shows that one of the models featured scooped-out coves behind both the front and the rear wheels. Notice also the exhaust pipe protruding through the fender, behind the rear wheel. At this stage the rims around the headlights were still painted, the wheel covers in preliminary form and the hood emblem small and accented by a chevron. Left and above, the various components of the fiberglass body as they were shown in GM's viewing complex.

show that GM indeed had a Gullwing on hand for inspiration and comparison.)

Seen in profile, the most obvious new element was the cove in the side panel, flaring back from the front wheel like a stylized cloud of fire and smoke. Similar designs had been seen before, on, for instance, the 1955 La Salle II Motorama show car and, even earlier, on Bertone's 1953 Arnolt Bristol coupe. But, as applied to the new Corvette, that cove became something of a trademark. Photographs, found in the GM files, show full-scale mock-ups featuring shorter coves behind the front as well as the rear wheel. Obviously, the single, long cove won.

From the rear, the elimination of the old rocket ship taillights created a smooth look with the new lights recessed in attractive, scoop-shaped bezels that did not interrupt the flowing line.

The overall form was clean and homogenous, and, especially from the front, aggressive looking. The three-quarter front view, with the somewhat overweight rear obscured, was an especially flattering angle. While criticizing the heaviness of the rear, one must at the same time complain about the small, nonfunctional air scoops on top of the fenders, just ahead of the windshield. It was the beginning of an unfortunate trend of make-believe embellishments that would escalate on future models. On the other hand, visually and historically, those details are a part of what makes this era so memorable. If the scoops had only been real! They were first seen on the original 1953 Motorama Corvette, but had vanished on the production model. The scoops weren't there on the 1956 preproduction mock-up either. Then, at the last minute, they showed up again. The chrome strip outlining the shape of the cove on the side panel was another last-minute addition.

I squeeze in behind the wheel of collector Waldo Adams' all-restored, show-condition 1957. The interior looks the same as in the old model, but the seats are now covered with the waffle-pattern vinyl. The light-beige interior

(continued on overleaf)

Not only one of the best looking Corvettes ever, the 1957 was also one of the best performing. The reason was fuel injection. The Cascade Green Survivor featured in these photographs, chassis number E57S102924, owned by Waldo Adams of Laguna Hills, California, has the most unusual and desirable option combination, fuel-injected 283 bhp and four-speed transmission.

contrasts nicely with the Cascade Green exterior. The steering wheel is still big, but it has been redesigned, looking very racy with its three drilled-out spokes. The driving position still adheres to the close-to-the-wheel attitude.

I start it up. It comes to life with a deep, rumbling, big-engine sound. I reach for the stick. One is up to the left. Two is down. Three is up to the right. And four is down. Yes, four! Waldo's is one of the few 1957s with the combination of four-speed and fuel injection. I press the gas pedal, lightly, and let go of the clutch, slowly, carefully.

"Pop it! Step on it!" Waldo calls out from the seat beside me, obviously willing to let me experience what his pride and joy is all about.

I do as he says. I step on it. And I pop it. Off it goes! No more motor boat like the 1953! No, sir! This one sounds as good as it goes. First there is that loud hissing from the fuel injection. It comes like the sound from when you open up the nozzle of a hose on a fire engine. Then there's the roar. And the vibration. And the smell of aromatic gases; odors from gasoline and exhaust, with some burning rubber mixed in, flow through the cockpit. I shift to second. Off it goes again. Bouncing. Leaping. Sliding. It feels like it wants to get away: like it's wrestling itself out of the grip of my hands. Beast! It's that famous, or infamous, wildness of these early Corvettes!

"It takes getting used to." Waldo shouts over the roar. "But once you do, it's a fun car to drive! Pop the clutch in third. But be careful. It can fishtail!"

I decide not to exercise that option. In fact there isn't enough road. Nor is there enough road for fourth. I brake and come to a standstill at the wayside. The 283 rumbles calmly, as if nothing had happened. Of course, I know that the juices still flow fast inside that chunk of iron, just as the blood flows fast inside my veins.

"Now I know why they didn't need those rocket ship taillights anymore," I say.

"How is that?" Waldo wonders.

"Instead of looking like a rocket, it goes like a rocket!"

A prototype fitted with a Duntov-modified engine and new 1956 body panels was brought to Daytona Beach in early January. Above, John Fitch distorts the image on the film as he speeds by. Driven by Zora Arkus-Duntov, the car reached 150 mph. But Duntov had something much more exciting up his sleeve: the SS racer. It made its debut at Sebring in the spring of 1957. Left, Juan Fangio tests the "mule." Lower right, cockpit and engine of actual SS. Upper right, Piero Taruffi at the wheel during the race, which, for the SS, ended after 23 laps.

Double-Lights, Double-Good...

In 1960, players of The Big Game make significant moves to improve their positions and realize their goals.

Elvis Presley returns from his Army exile in Europe. His new release, *Are You Lonesome Tonight?*, shoots to the top of the charts. Cassius Clay wins an Olympic gold medal in Rome. Soon afterward he turns professional.

De Gaulle has become president. Castro has overthrown Batista. Khrushchev is firmly in power. And Kennedy wins the presidential election with a narrow margin.

At General Motors, William L. Mitchell is now head of styling. For several years he has been toying with ideas for a new Corvette. One such experiment is the 1957 Q-Corvette. Although its time has not yet come, it nevertheless turns out to be the embryo of a future Corvette. The same styling ideas are further refined in a new sports racer, first seen in 1959. Because of an agreement between the automakers not to engage in racing, Mitchell develops and enters this car on his own. It can't display the Corvette badge. It's instead named Sting Ray. The first year reveals serious shortcomings, but as these are corrected, the 1960 season sees the sleek silver machine capturing the SCCA championship.

Another personality at GM is also making a steady advance. He is Zora Arkus-Duntov, an engineer with a uniquely made-to-order background. His energy, for the first few years applied to improving the existing models, is then focused on the Q-Corvette, but as it becomes

Even before the 1956 model arrived in the showrooms, the styling staff had been busy at work to prepare for the changes that would be implemented in 1958. Left, the double lights and triple grilles as they looked on January 17, 1956. Notice that the chrome strip around the cove continues almost all the way to the headlights. Also notice the different bumper alternatives. Above, the wide chrome bands on the trunk lid are tried out. Upper right, the front is getting closer to its final form but still has a mesh grille. Both pictures are dated January 30. Lower right, the final look, dated August 7.

DAYTON
1-30-56

clear that this effort is premature, he returns to the existing Corvette, specifically the 1960 model. His labors result in increased performance and improved handling.

In spite of the ban on racing, the enthusiasts at GM, with Duntov in the lead, find ways to keep the Corvette competitive. The secret lies in the option packages. With the fuel injected 283, the positraction axle, the four-speed transmisson, the heavy duty brakes and suspension, and the twentyfour-gallon fuel tank, the Corvette is ready for almost anything!

In addition to the succes of the Sting Ray, Corvettes capture first in class in the Twelve Hours of Sebring, eighth overall at Le Mans, as well as another SCCA championship.

In Middleburg, Virginia, another player of The Big Game is quietly laying the foundation for a future career in the automotive field. In 1960, William Gray is ten years old. Already as a two-year-old he amazes people by being able to distinguish between the various makes that pass on the street in front of his parents' home. As a ten-year-old, none of the facts and feats of the Corvette elude him.

In 1958, the Corvette receives its share of the superficial embellishments showered on automobiles at this time. In addition to the already fake scoops on the fenders, it also gets fake louvers on the hood and fake vents in the side panels as well as twin headlights, triple grilles, and double chrome strips on the rear deck lid. Thanks to Mitchell the act is cleaned up quite a bit for 1960 and, together with the improvements resulting from Duntov's work, it is now a most impressive machine.

This 1960 Corvette proves too much of a temptation to a man in La Jolla; he becomes an owner, in spite of the almost five-thousand-dollar price tag. He pays 16 dollars extra to get the cove painted Ermine White. He opts for the fuel-injected 275 hp, 283 ci engine, costing 485 dollars, the four-speed transmission, 188 dollars, and the whitewall tires, costing an ad-
(continued on overleaf)

Some say it was over-decorated. But it is easy to see why, in spite of, or thanks to, the dual lights and triple grilles, the 1960 Corvette made every head turn! Owner William Gray of La Jolla, California, bought this beauty, chassis number 00867S103004, from its first owner. A nine-thousand-dollar paint-job, part of a cost-no-object restoration, makes this Survivor sparkle in front of a not-so-still Pacific.

ditional 32 dollars.

He keeps his prize possession in perfect condition. But not like a show car. After all, he drives it. As the years go by, and new models come out, he still likes the good old 1960. He never falls for the temptation to change things, add things, not even to paint it.

When William Gray turns fifteen he buys his first car, a 1948 Buick Sedanette. At seventeen, he buys his first new car, a 1963 Chevrolet Impala Super Sport. Both cars are bought with money he has earned himself. During the following years, spent studying business administration and marketing, cars remain a central part of his life, but only as a hobby. In 1975, after having made his money in real estate, he decides to devote himself full time to cars, opening a showroom in San Diego, featuring classic and special-interest cars.

The same year, he also becomes aware of that certain 1960 Corvette rolling on the streets of nearby La Jolla. He locates the owner and befriends him.

It takes five years until the man is ready to sell. He realizes that he will never be able to restore the car the way William Gray will.

William Gray has never before owned a Corvette. But he remembers the year of 1960. He wants this one for himself. To keep. And he wants to do it right, in every detail.

"I don't think I should advertize how much I spent on restoring this car," Gray says. "But I can tell you that the paint job alone cost nine thousand dollars!"

"Can you really justify investing that much in a Corvette?" I wonder.

"Yes. To me, the satisfaction lays in seeing a car brought back to its original condition without having to compromise. Besides, based on my experience in the business, I feel the Corvette is still one of the biggest sleepers around."

He says it with a conviction that makes me feel that he knows what he is talking about. And he most likely does. For William Gray has a record of doing things right, as well as doing the right thing.

These never-before-published photographs provide a fascinating glimpse of what goes on behind the curtains of secrecy. On this page, interior shots from one of the design studios, dated December 9, 1955. The unfinished mockup is an Oldsmobile dream car, the Golden Rocket. Its headlights and grille provided the ideas for the 1958 Corvette. Opposite page, these photos, dated December 29, were taken in the new viewing complex. The mockup is ready to be seen by the brass. Notice the split rear window and the roof panels that opened with the door. Present was also the new Corvette and a sampling of competitors.

The Right Stuff.

Nineteen-sixty-two was a year of milestones. John Glenn became the first American to orbit the earth. The Telstar communications satellite was launched and began relaying transatlantic broadcasts. The Missile Crisis brought the world to the brink of nuclear war.

Marilyn Monroe died. John Steinbeck won the Nobel Prize. And James Meredith was admitted to the University of Mississippi.

In the world of Corvette, one more year would pass before a milestone appeared. Although, to a lesser degree, the last year of each generation should also be considered milestones; the 1962 was indeed a last.

The basic body style had not been altered, but an important change had been made the year before, when the tail section had received a new look. It took its inspiration from the 1957 Q-Corvette with its hip-level crease, running all around the car. This look was further refined on the 1959 Sting Ray racer. And, as we know, it would ultimately end up on the new Corvette. In fact, in retrospect, it looks like a carefully orchestrated plan to educate the public; first came the Q-Corvette, then the Sting Ray sports racer, then the XP-700, then the 1961 redesign, then the Shark and finally, the culmination: the production-version Sting Ray.

But the 1961 face lift, or should we say bottom lift, incorporated this treatment only at the rear. A positive result was that the heaviness of the old tail section was eliminated. A negative effect was that the front and rear no longer harmonized. Nevertheless, the new look allowed the

Man of many coats! Zora Arkus-Duntov was the name most significantly linked with the continuous progress of the Corvette. He brought to GM an expertise in both racing and engineering; knowledge gained in Europe. Above, Zora is keeping warm while waiting for his turn behind the wheel of the Porsche he brought to a class win at Le Mans in 1954. Left, at Sebring in 1961. Right, showing off the ZL-1 to reporters at a Phoenix drag strip in 1969. Far right, a different coat was donned during sessions at GM, where he was often called upon to argue the case for all of America's true sports car enthusiasts.

basic style to stay in production.

While Mitchell had instigated these alterations to the body, Arkus-Duntov had not been neglecting the mechanics, although both men and their staffs by now were seriously occupied with a successor. In fact, as is true in most cases, the longer a basic model runs, the more it tends to be improved. At least, this seems to be true when it comes to the mechanics; the 1962 model is no exception. For this continued progress, one must credit a man who, through his determination, became one of the most forceful movers behind the Corvette: Zora Arkus-Duntov.

Looking back, tracing the events that led Duntov to GM, it seems more like a coincidence than a plan that this man, possessing the perfect credentials for the job, would in fact end up being hired by Research and Development.

Zora Arkus-Duntov was born in Belgium while his Russian parents completed their schooling in that country. The year was 1910. In the post-revolution years we find the family in Leningrad. But life in Russia must not have been what it promised; they moved to Germany.

As is often the case with creative minds, school does not seem to agree with them. This was the case with young Zora. Not until he began studying engineering, first in Leningrad, then in Berlin, did he seem to find his purpose. His final work was in the field of supercharging.

During the prewar years Zora launched a career in engineering, cultivating contacts in Belgium, France and Germany, working on projects as diverse as motorcycles and locomotives. The outbreak of war put a halt to these activities. The early capitulation of France found him in that country's air force. An American visa unexpectedly brought him to New York, where he was enrolled in the war effort, designing aircraft engines. After the war, Zora started a company that specialized in speed equipment. His Ardun overhead valve conversion became a popular item. In the early fifties we find Duntov tied to Allard in England as a consultant. In 1952 and 1953, he drove Allards at Le Mans.

(continued on overleaf)

No teeth in the grille. Four round rear lights. These are some of the changes introduced in 1961. In 1962, the side vents were redesigned, as can be seen in the photograph above, featuring Pat Connells' of Costa Mesa, California, fuel-injected 327. This Survivor, chassis number 20867S112637, represents the last of the body style; a style etched into the eye of every American car enthusiast; an image as American as that of a baseball batting cage.

It was during that time a friend encouraged him to make contact with GM. A letter from Ed Cole, the chief engineer, and later a visit to Detroit, ultimately led to his hiring. Earlier in 1953, before he began at GM, Duntov had seen the first Corvette at the New York premier showing. He seems to have been impressed by its looks more than its performance. This impression was confirmed later when he had a chance to test-drive it. Although he was not involved in the Corvette program at that time, through his background and inclination, he was inevitably drawn to it. Covertly he began to suggest changes which resulted in improved steering and suspension.

In 1957, Duntov became the chief engineer of the Corvette project and could devote himself wholeheartedly to the work his previous experiences had groomed him for, gradually upgrading the production models, but also creating a most exciting sports racing car, the SS. Unfortunately, the SS saw action only once. Its potential was obvious. Both Juan Fangio and Stirling Moss tested the car and were impressed. But there were shortcomings. Regrettably, before these could be corrected, the ban on racing put a halt to all further activities. One of the planned assignments for the SS had been an all-out attack on Le Mans.

It is obvious that Duntov had in mind to establish a reputation for the Corvette that, if he had been allowed to follow through, could have given even more glory to the marque. It would have been a picture to savor for the future, to have seen the Corvette SS cross the finish line at Le Mans in 1957 as the winner!

Fortunately, Duntov was successful in persuading management to let him continue to develop those exciting options for the road cars. For 1962, this took the form of an enlarged engine, the 327, with the highest power output yet, 360 hp.

Just as John Glenn had what it took to make that first flight a success, Zora Arkus-Duntov had what it took to turn the Corvette into a real sports car. The right stuff.

The touch of Duntov began to make itself felt on the racing circuits in 1956. Opposite page, upper right, hard-charging Dick Thompson and Paul O'Shea duel at Sebring, with the Corvette the winner. On this page, left, Bob Bondurant entering turn six at Riverside in 1960. John Fitch and Bob Grossman drove to an honorable eighth overall at Le Mans in 1960. Above, the same year, Lilley and Gamble crossed the finish line in tenth place, but had not covered minimum distance. Opposite page, center, the start at Sebring in 1961. Bottom, Elkhart Lake 1961. Yenko and Lother, number 11, won.

63

Of Sting Rays and Flying Saucers...

It makes a lot of difference where and when you see a car. Crowded parking lots and busy downtown streets certainly don't work to a car's advantage. Even showrooms, often cramped and badly lighted, seldom provide the proper setting for viewing.

The open road is a good place to see a car. Especially if you stand at the wayside for the sole purpose of taking in the image of the car as it passes, as I have done on many occasions.

One of the most memorable of such events took place in Northern Italy. It was a narrow road that curved its way up a hillside. From where I stood I could only see a short straightaway and the sharp, slanting curve that led into it. The car was a 1929 Alfa Romeo 1750 with a beautiful sound that echoed between the hills as it worked its way up the incline, decelerating, shifting, accelerating. When the red Alfa finally appeared, sliding through the curve, there was no other time or place when and where it could have looked better.

The time is early morning. The place is a gravel pit in York, Pennsylvania. Three individuals inhabit the otherwise deserted location: a 1963 Sting Ray, its owner George Wagman, and myself, camera equipped as always

George got "the bug" in 1976 when he visited a friend who still owned a 1956 Corvette he had bought new. A new Corvette did not provide the nostalgia he had originally sought; a 1966 coupe became the first in a long string of older ones. Best from a show point of view, was a red-on-red

1963. That coupe, on one occasion, brought him Best Paint, Best in Class and Best of Show! The bug had bit him to a degree that he finally owned ten Corvettes. By then he realized that it was too much. He couldn't enjoy them all. He decided to sell. The one to keep, curiously enough, but typical of a true enthusiast, was the dark blue coupe now standing at the bottom of the gravel pit, not the restored red one, but the all-original one, the one that could be driven without worry.

The sun is barely up, and it's not going to reach the bottom plane of the pit for several hours yet. That's the way we want it. But we do need stronger illumination from above, from the sky. As soon as the car has been placed in the right spot in relation to the anticipated light and the sloping mountains of gravel, looking through the camera, I know this is another of those perfect settings. The dark blue coupe is complemented by the cool blueness of the still unlit gravel.

William L. Mitchell was born in Cleveland, Ohio. The year was 1912. His parents soon moved to Greenville, Pennsylvania, where his father became a Buick dealer. It was not unexpected then that young Billy quickly became a certified car enthusiast. During the summers of his high school years he worked as an office boy in a large New York advertising agency. This awakened his interest in commercial art. This period also refined his interest in automobiles as he spent many of his off-hours visiting the elegant showrooms of the best of the European classics of the day. Upon graduation he joined the firm full time.

The sons of the firm's owner happened to be consummate sports car enthusiasts. Bill often joined them in their road racing adventures. He did not only drive the cars, he also recorded the action in sketches. Some of these were seen by a friend of Harley Earl, in charge of styling at GM. Bill was encouraged to send his work to Earl, and in the fall of 1935 he was hired.

He must have shown an unusual amount of flair for his job; at the age of twenty-four he was *(continued on overleaf)*

William L. Mitchell, for two decades vice president in charge of General Motors Styling, loved cars with a passion. To the left, he is seen in one of the studios. On the table are scale models of GM experimentals, Firebird I, II and III. In the background the full-size clay model of the Firebird IV receives careful attention. This page, top, Mitchell is seen with the 1959 Sting Ray racer and a production version 1963 Sting Ray. Above, the 1961 Shark, together with the racer, heralding the new Corvette look. Right, "The Flying Dentist," Dick Thompson, in the Sting Ray racer.

Corvette's finest hour? Many connoisseurs feel the split-window coupe of 1963 is just that! As it turned out, it was just a one-year feature, making it especially unique. With its fuel-injected 327, four-speed transmission, side-mount exhaust, this Daytona Blue Survivor, chassis number 30837S110222, owned by George Wagman of York, Pennsylvania, represents the best of the best!

promoted to head the Cadillac program. He proceeded to create many outstanding designs, among them the 1938 Sixty Special, and the 1941, introducing the "egg-crate" grille.

When Earl retired in 1958, Bill Mitchell was chosen to succeed him. A long row of superb designs were created under his reign, starting with the Riviera, and continuing with such milestones as the Toronado, the Eldorado, the Camaro and Firebird.

But his special pet was always the Corvette. This could be expected from a true sports car enthusiast, one of the few to inhabit the vast organization. Through many battles with the "bean counters," as Mitchell called them, he and the few faithful managed to keep the Corvette alive and exciting.

George and I still wait for that perfect light. In the meantime, the shape of that Sting Ray becomes the focusing point. As I try, in my mind, to relate the basic look to other designs, for almost nothing is entirely new under the sun, I recall the 1952 Alfa Romeo Disco Volante, by Touring. It had that same hip-level crease running all around the body. The object was to create a smooth, flat shape, as low as possible, like a saucer turned upside down (Disco Volante means Flying Saucer), and then place protrusions for the wheels in the four corners. Mitchell might very well have been inspired by this design when he drew his 1959 sports racer. Although, he made the lines sharper, crisper, and the crease more pronounced, giving the Sting Ray a look all its own. Mitchell's ingenious solution for the headlights of the production Sting Ray added further to that quality.

When the right light comes, it comes suddenly, and it never lasts long. In the rush of searching for the right camera angles I have the opportunity to discover the many beautiful and exciting facets of the Sting Ray style. I find that Bill Mitchell indeed lived up to his own philosophy. He felt that a car must have enough areas of interest so that every time you look at it you will see something new.

Much of the work that goes on inside the design studios never reaches production. Naturally, the final look is not arrived upon without trials and errors, illustrated by the unique series of photos reproduced on these pages. Opposite page, upper row, a possible replacement for the 1961 model. The date is February 4, 1959. Only the tail section made it. Lower row, a couple of suggestions for treatment of the lights, dated April 26, 1961. Fortunately, they did not make it. Above, one of the full-size clay models after having served its purpose. Left, a suggested design for the air-conditioning outlet.

Reflections From the Cockpit.

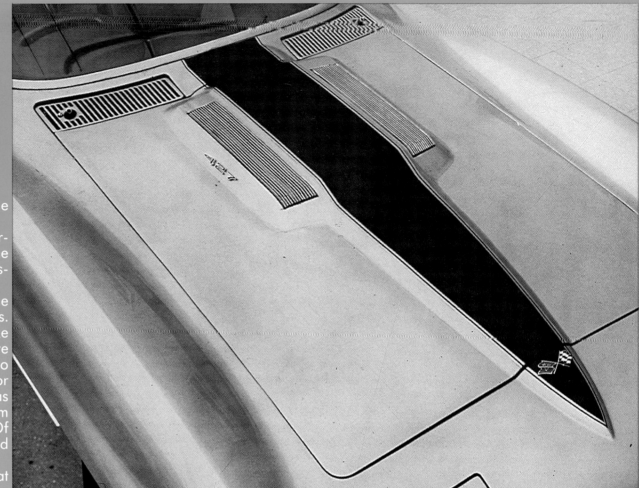

Of all Corvettes, which is the most rare? The most beautiful? The most desirable?

Questions like these are asked whenever Corvette enthusiasts get together. Ferrari, Porsche and Mercedes people all have the same questions. (Cobra enthusiasts have it easy.)

To come up with answers that satisfy everyone is impossible. Sure, there are certain basic facts. But facts can be interpreted differently. Just like two religious organizations can have opposite views of the same text, the Corvette faith also leaves room for individual opinions. Some, for instance, may think of the dual headlights as being beautiful, while others may think of them as being horrible. Who's to say what's right? (Of course, there's something, called "educated taste.")

Here are my personal reflections (for what they're worth).

The award for Most Unique Corvette must go to the 53. Obviously, with only 300 built, that category is simple. The number of cars made is just right. Not too few, which would have made the model too obscure. Not too many, which would have made it too easy to obtain. A 55 with the first V-8 is also unique, but it certainly can't top a 53. After all, the 53 represents the beginning of it all. You can't beat that!

With its lowly six-cylinder engine and its unsporty Powerglide transmission, the 53 wasn't outstanding mechanically. On the other hand, it was very good looking, but would certainly not qualify as the best looking of all Corvettes. It seemed overweight. Too wide. And then there

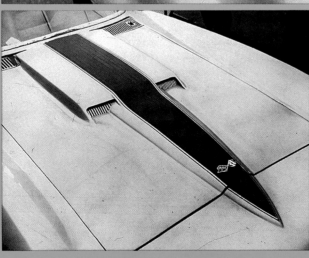

With the introduction of the new Mark IV engine in 1965, a larger hood bulge was required. As can be seen in the photos on this page, various designs were considered. The alternative chosen is barely visible in the photo on the opposite page, top. This car is fitted with the 1967 type knock-off aluminum wheels with its wingless nuts. The 1967 shown in the photo to the right is fitted with wheels of a new design introduced that year. Curiously enough, at this point, the wheels are still sporting three-winged nuts that later had to be removed, due to new safety regulations.

were the rocket ship taillights. Embellishments unbecoming a sports car.

Deciding which model is worthy of the award for Most Beautiful Corvette isn't easy. Using the method of elimination might help.

The first generation is already out of contention, as indicated above.

How about the second generation? Well, toward the end, 61 and 62, there was the unfortunate combination of two different styling philosophies (when the Sting Ray type tail was introduced). In the middle, 58 to 60, the cars looked like Christmas trees, with all their louvers, lights and vents. The early years, 56 and 57, were very good looking, but the rear was too heavy, too prominent. Try to visualize the stinger section of a bee. That's the look. (To some this may be just what they like!) The curves were just a little too round back there. Also, the stylists had not bothered to taper the fenders (looking at them from above now), like they did on, for instance, the Jaguar XK 120.

The fourth generation, 68 to 82, was characterized by a continous change of shapes. Although the basic design was always exciting looking, the surfaces undulated too much. There was a feeling of exaggeration in the lines. The coke-bottle effect, caused by the shape of the rocker panels, didn't help matters. To me, there was also something unpleasant about that sugar-scoop design behind the rear window. The design looked better as a fastback, as seen in the Mako Shark and the Manta Ray. With the introduction of the integrated front and rear bumpers, the overhangs became too great. With the arrival of the fastback, things looked better, but by then it had all been around too long.

The 1984 Corvette may very well turn out to be the most beautiful. I wouldn't be surprised. But it's really too early to tell. There needs to be a period of time for the design to mature.

That leaves only the third generation. The original Sting Ray. But what year to choose? The first year, 63, had the split window. Certainly a unique element. But it also had the fake louvers
(continued on overleaf)

Sting Rays also looked good in convertible form. Actually, coupes were outsold two to one in 1965. This Silver Pearl copy, chassis number 19467S100230, selected from the inventory of Southern California Classics in La Jolla, shows off its simple, clean shape. If anyone doubted that the Sting Ray meant business, all he had to do was to look at the badges, by now representing real racing victories.

und vents. The last year, 67, had none of these. Even the superfluous badges had been removed. Now it's finally as clean and pure as it should have been in the first place. So, coupe or roadster? The roadster is certainly superbly balanced. There's a perfect harmony between front and rear. But it lacks the character of the coupe. The coupe has that tapering fastback.

So, by using the unscientific method of subjective evaluation combined with the scientific method of elimination, the Most Beautiful Corvette has been selected: The winner is the 1967 Sting Ray coupe.

How about Most Desirable Corvette?

To the east I have the San Diego Bay. In the corner of my eye, I can see the gray silhouettes of the warships anchored over by the Naval Station. To the west, immediately beside me, I have the sands of Coronado Beach and the waves of the Pacific. Straight ahead, my eyes catch the tower-and-turret outline of the old Del Coronado Hotel. Off to the right is the concrete-and-steel rainbow of the Bay Bridge, and beyond it, the San Diego skyline. Surrounding me, I have a sleek silver roadster, its body shivering from the strain of acceleration, a lovely, deafeningly loud sound of rapid-fire explosions rising from the off-road exhaust pipes, mounted just below the doors. The engine is finnicky, like a race horse; only when I keep the revs high does want to run right, the fuel injection coming on in a hissing rush then. And, topping it off is that wind shooting by, warm, soothing, bringing with it that salty, intoxicating smell of ocean.

So, how about the Most Desirable Corvette? Well, here's where anyone can have a say. This is the individual's choice.

My choice? A 1965 Sting Ray (for independent suspension and disc brakes) with the biggest, fuel injected engine and close-ratio box (for acceleration and shifting pleasure).

Oh, yes, it has to be a roadster. Naturally, for open-air motoring and well-balanced, simple lines!

In 1962 Duntov was pushing yet another racing venture. It was the ill-fated Grand Sport. One hundred units were to have been built, allowing GT homologation. With five cars completed, management axed the project; the cars were sold to privateers. During the 1963 Nassau Speed Week three Grand Sports gave a show of what could have been; by 1965 it was no longer competitive—to the right, Delmo Johnson finished far back in the field at Sebring. Left, Dick Thompson in a Z06 Corvette at Marlboro in January 1963. Above, a design study shown at the 1964 Auto Show in New York.

The Quest for the Best.

Providence, Rhode Island.
October 22. Afternoon.
Raining all day. Saw the Corvette this morning. Best I've ever seen. Met the owner, Anthony Pate. Has service station. Father had it before him. Anthony added nice new building. Sells Corvettes and other special-interest cars out of it. Used to work for his father at the station. That's when he first got interested in Corvettes. Used to service a 53 for years. Got to know it pretty well. Owned a 65 at that time. Bought new. But didn't appreciate it then. Was into motorcycles. Competed in motocross for ten years. Ran races all over New England. Corvette appreciation came later. In 1974. Began looking through *Hemmings*. Checked ads locally. Looked at many cars. But couldn't find one that was good enough. Kept searching. Saw ad one day: 1967 Corvette, 400 hp, tri-carb, four-speed, air, redline tires, bolt-on wheels. Sounded just like the kind of car he had been wanting. But when he went to check it: junk! Couldn't find a car that was good enough. Not until Brainerd. At the Corvette show. Now he knew the good cars existed. Met Chip Miller there.

Midnight.

Went with Anthony to Italian restaurant for dinner. Had ravioli. Talked motocross. Haven't done that for years. Turned out Anthony knew all the names I knew. Who was World Champion that year? Who was the best BSA driver? Fun game. Small world. Talked location for shooting the Corvette too. Said he would go anywhere. Has brand new, covered trailer. Distance

The 1967 marked the high point of the Sting Ray series. Superfluous ornamentation had been removed and there were also various other improvements of a subtle nature. Even though the coupe must be considered the foremost example of the Sting Ray style, the roadster had a superbly balanced look, especially with the optional hardtop fitted, as seen in these photographs. This roadster has the standard wheels. Rim width had been increased to six inches, improving both looks and handling. The interior had received new seats and the handbrake had been relocated to a more logical location between them.

doesn't matter. But said he wouldn't take it out in the rain. That's understandable.

October 23. Noon.
Still raining. Have been looking for location in spite of. Having hard time finding what I want. Want something special. Something worthy of that black beauty.
Evening.
Think I found a good spot. Boat yard. Saw several America's Cup entrants. Ted Turner's *Tenacious* also. Some of world's best boats. One of world's best Corvettes. Could be good. Also looked closely at the car this afternoon. Incredible restoration. Chip Miller owned it before Anthony. Bought it from original owner. Tuxedo Black with black vinyl interior and red hood stripe. Has all the right options. The 435 hp 427 ci engine, transistor ignition, positraction rear axle, four-speed close ratio transmission, special front and rear suspension, side mount exhaust, tinted glass, special cast aluminum bolt-on wheels, redline tires, AM-FM radio. Owner pampered it. Paint was great. Everything was great. Didn't need restoration. Just one thing wrong: Main cross-member had been butchered to make room for four-inch pipes. Chip took it to Ken Heckert to get that taken care of. Body had to be pulled off. Once body was off, one thing led to another. In the end Chip had a full-fledged show car. Anthony saw it both before and after. When it was done, he knew he had finally found what he had been looking for.
Midnight.
Had dinner with Anthony. Cannelloni. He showed snap shots of restoration. Frame looks so clean you could have displayed it in an operating room. Painted exactly the way they did it at the factory. Even has the original markings restenciled on the frame and elsewhere. Talked motocross too. That Swede, what's his name, he was good! Bill Nilsson! Right. Did you ever see him? Yes, saw him in Sweden. Strange thing about him, he never looked fast. He was so smooth. It's still raining. Raindrops play the
(continued on overleaf)

Black on black. Tuxedo Black, no less. And a little touch of red, like the rose in the lapel. How subtle! Because this is not the one to take to the theater. This is the real brute, the last and the fastest of the Sting Rays. Of course, if you are a bit late, five seconds to sixty can make a difference. This 1967, chassis number 194377S111704, owned by Anthony Pate of Providence, Rhode Island, is so perfect, it must be one of the finest around.

drums on the motel room window. Melancholic motel music. On the news they say it's going to clear up tomorrow. Let's hope so.

October 24. Morning.
Not raining. But doesn't look safe. Able to talk Anthony into going shooting anyway.
Afternoon.
Was wrong about the boat yard. No good. Too busy looking. Difficult to place car right in relation to boats. Also, owner of yard complained about noise from the Corvette. Sound is terrific. Terrificallly beautiful. That guy is no enthusiast. I guess sails and motors don't mix! Got one good shot only. Was working on another when it started to sprinkle. Barely got the Corvette inside the trailer when it began pouring down. Offered to help Anthony wipe off a few drops. But he wanted to do it himself.
Midnight.
Had dinner with Anthony. Veal marinara. Talked motocross. It's raining. On the news they say its going to be overcast tomorrow, but no rain. Phoned Anthony about emergency location. Have to move on tomorrow. Can't wait any longer. Have to be in Detroit. Meeting with Jerry Palmer at GM already set up far in advance. Need a location badly. Don't want to take just anything. No golf course. Not in front of fancy house. Not that conventional stuff. Something typically American! How about Coca-Cola trucks? Anthony says. I have a friend over at the bottling plant. I'm sure he'll let us do it there. I'll call him, Anthony says. Anthony calls back. Friend on vacation. Decide to try it anyway.

October 25. Midnight.
Coca-Cola location worked fine. Did all shooting in half an hour because it started to rain. Turned out fine though. Things go better with Coke! But didn't get to drive it. Close ratio box! Over four hundred horses! Would have loved it! My bad luck. Anthony's good luck. Should have left earlier but wife Susan served spaghetti with homemade meat sauce in front of TV while Anthony and I watched motocross.

For a long time it was the common opinion that the price level of the Sting Rays did not warrant too thorough a restoration of these cars. But sometimes a market has to be tested before a breakthrough will take place. Some of the foremost experts and enthusiasts on the East Coast were involved in the project captured in snapshots on these pages. (The car is also the feature of this section's color photos). Chip Miller was the owner, Ken Heckert the restorer, both of York, Pennsylvania, and Anthony Pate of Providence, Rhode Island, purchased the completed car. The three proved that "a quest for the best" always pays off.

Wildest of the Wild.

It's the kind of idea that pops into my mind, uninvited, unwanted, but intriguing.

In the July 1969 issue of the now-defunct *Car Life* magazine, the editors reported on the "Wildest Corvette Test Yet." It took place on the dragstrip and road-racing course of Mel Larson's Sportsland, outside Phoenix, Arizona. There were two stars present. One, a pre-production ZL-1. The other, its creator, Zora Arkus-Duntov. He recorded a quarter-mile time of 12.1 seconds, driving leisurely.

Now, as I stand here on the tarmack of Richmond Racetrack, Virginia, site of the annual Richmond 400, talking with Wayne Walker, admiring his yellow ZL-1, the idea knocks on my brain again: Should we try to beat that time?

It wouldn't be quite scientific, of course. All I have is my wristwatch chronometer. At Phoenix they had the dragstrip timing setup. Another problem: The straightaway here is probably just barely quarter of a mile long, which would force us to enter the turn at about 120 mph.

Also a problem: We only have permission to take pictures. No racing. But I figure we would be able to squeeze in a couple of fast laps without anyone noticing. However, I decide not to mention the idea to Wayne yet.

Duntov's ZL-1 started out as a stock L-88. Its engine was replaced by the ZL-1 unit; its aluminum block weighed 100 pounds less. Otherwise it was, basically, identical to the L-88, using the same aluminum heads and intake manifolds. The car was actually prepared for racing, with everything unnecessary removed: headlights,

The Mako Shark II, opposite page, was very much the expression of Bill Mitchell's taste. He was fascinated with the shark them and carried it through to the extreme with such things as a paint job that copied the graduated tones of that prowler of the deep. The same basic theme is evident in the full-scale mockup pictured to the right. The photos were taken on December 2, 1964. In my own opinion, this is how the new Corvette should have looked! Lack of rearwo visibility probably killed it. Left, a photo of more recent date, sometime in 19. shows an alternative approvach to the racing striping that was to adorn the ZL-1.

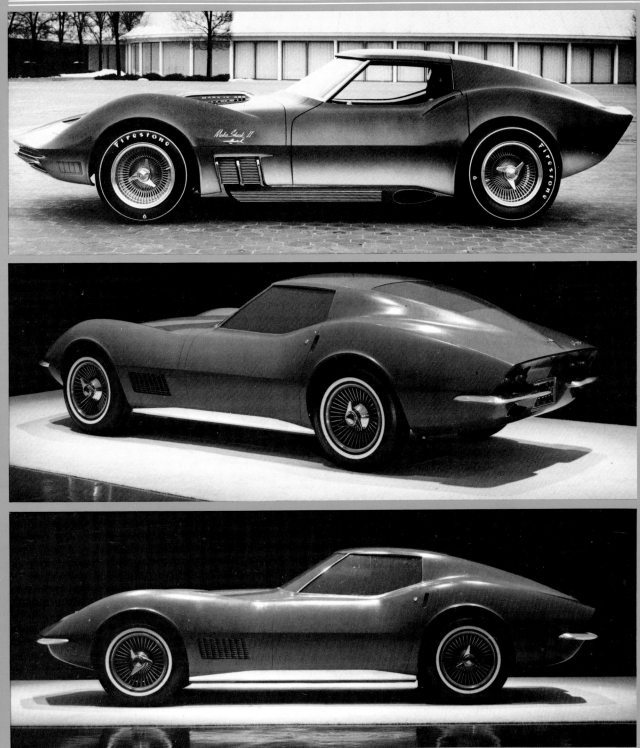

bumpers, upholstery, spare tire, heater and so on. Weight was down to 2,900 pounds.

Wayne's ZL-1 is what Duntov made available to the customer, in 1969, as part of the option list. For some reason, only two were assembled. Wayne's ZL-1 is quite a bit heavier than the one driven by Duntov at Phoenix; it has all the standard features of a street Corvette, albeit minus radio, fan shroud and a few other things. But Duntov's car had the 3.70 gearing. Wayne's has the 4.11. That, plus some aggressive clutching and shifting, I figure, might give us the edge, should we decide to try to beat Zora's time. There's that blasted idea again!

Wayne's ZL-1 must be one of the most rare Corvettes in existence. Not only as it stands completed today, the only one known to exist, but also the way it got here.

It was originally ordered as a company car by an engineer at the St. Louis Corvette plant. The sticker was $10,771. When the engineer moved on, the ZL-1 was left for his successor, who arranged for it to be sold. It ended up on the lot of a Chevrolet dealership in Richmond, sitting there for quite a while. Finally, a friend of Wayne bought it. On the first night out he blew the engine. Next day he took it back to the dealer to have it replaced under warranty. When the new engine arrived, the friend decided to use it in his drag boat instead. At some point, the blown engine disappeared from the dealership. And was lost.

The yellow Corvette, with the distinctive black racing stripe on the hood, sat with a for-sale sign at the friend's gas station for a couple of years. Nobody would want to pay $3,000 for a Corvette without an engine, Wayne remembers thinking. A 454 was put into it. The car then went back to the original dealer. After sitting there for a while, it was finally sold. And lost, too.

The years passed. One day in 1976, Wayne read an article that mentioned the rarity of the L-88 and ZL-1 options, and he had a sudden flashback to the ZL-1 his friend had once owned. He looked him up and it turned out that the car
(continued on overleaf)

Sure, the black stripe on the hood doesn't mean much, unless you know what it stands for. What does it stand for? The ultimate! Simply, the most unique, the most powerful, the most fascinating Corvette ever offered to the public, the ultimate beast: the ZL-1. Wayne Walker (driving the locomotive, for a change) of Mechanicsville, Virginia, owns this 1969, chassis number 194379S729219, one of two built, and the only one left.

was still in the area. Actually, just two blocks from where Wayne worked. After some convincing, he managed to buy it.

The task was now, as Wayne saw it, to find the right kind of engine. He finally managed to locate one in Pittsburg.

But, unexpectedly, out of the blue, Wayne got a call from a drag racer who had heard that Wayne was restoring the ZL-1. He said he had the original engine.

Now, having had the spectacular luck of finding the original engine, Wayne became serious about restoring the car. As soon as the ZL-1 was fitted, he took it out on the back roads, only to blow the engine. But, his enthusiasm was awakened. He decided to go back to square one, doing a total restoration of engine, frame and body. At that time, however, he had just started a new company, Zip Products, specializing in Corvette parts, and the ZL-1 again had to be placed on the back burner. A couple of years later, with the company off the ground and running smoothly, the project was tackled again. When completed, it captured a Gold at the 1981 Bloomington Corvette Corral.

The shooting is done now. Well, almost. We just need a few shots of the ZL-1 doing a drag-strip take-off. Vrooom! There's that ear-shattering, spine-tingling roar. The wheels are spinning. There's a cloud of blue smoke. The car is fishtailing. But Wayne has it under control. Off he goes, shooting on through turn one. As I stand there, absent-mindedly winding the film, looking at the ZL-1 accelerating down the straightaway, that stubborn idea crops up again. I decide to break it to him when he comes around.

He's coming out of turn four. Looking good. Sounding good. But, suddenly, I see smoke! Wayne slows down and comes to a stop. No, it's not smoke. It's steam. It's boiling!

So much for my idea. I don't seem to be able to lay my itching hands on a high-power Corvette. First, Anthony Pate's L-71, rained-out. Now, Wayne Walker's ZL-1, boiled-over. Someone out there doesn't want me to have any fun.

It's probably my Guardian Angel.

The most powerful option ever to be offered on the Corvette, the ZL-1, was shown to the editors of Car Life magazine early in 1969. Duntov himself took time out from his busy schedule to attend the event which took place at a drag strip in Phoenix. Bill Motta, Road & Track's art director, ably covered the occasion with his camera: Left, the ZL-1 at speed. Above, Duntov at the wheel. Right, Duntov in one of his many coats. Far right, top, shooting the breeze, flanked by the ZL-1 and gear. Bottom, a pack of Corvettes crowd the corner in one phase of the test, labeled "Wildest Corvette Test Yet!"

75

The Last Convertible.

The day has been clear and crisp, but windy. Now dusk has arrived and Marty and I turn to the horizon as a small plane comes in for landing, just in time to beat that last long light. The plane comes floating slightly sideways. A few rudder corrections compensate for the wind, and it lands on the short grassy field, bouncing as it touches the ground. This must be the only plane stationed here on this seemingly abandoned field a few miles south of East Berlin.

No, this is not the prologue of a spy novel. And we are not in East Berlin, Germany. We are in East Berlin, Pennsylvania. Marty is not an escaping Communist dignitary with the secret locations of missile bases on a microfilm hidden in his leather cap. He is the owner of a Flame Orange 1975 Corvette convertible, now parked in front of the hangar. And I am not the CIA station manager. I am the omnipresent photographer, here because of Marty and his car, one of the best of the last of the convertibles.

Why here? Well, when searching for a suitable background in a countryside dominated by barns, trees and fields, a lone hangar, its corrugated walls covered with black and white checkered squares — like the flag in the Corvette emblem — was too obviuous to ignore.

In 1975, with the disappearance of the convertible Corvette, a tradition disappeared with it. For 23 years there had always been an open Corvette. In fact, for the first three years, it was the only choice. Then, with the introduction of the 1956, a hardtop became available.

The new Corvette offered a variety of choices for the wind-in-the-hair enthusiast. The convertible top, above, was easy to operate and stowed neatly under its lid. The coupe had an unorthodox solution to blue-sky access; it was possible to remove not only two roof panels, right, top, but also the rear window, bottom, allowing almost unobstructed flow of air. The removable rear window was no longer available in 1973. Left, the one-piece roof panel of the 1965 Mako Shark was also planned for the 1968 production Corvette, but a last-minute change, delaying production, was required because of lack of rigidity.

When the third-generation Corvette was introduced, in 1963, the star of the show was the new coupe, the fastback Sting Ray.

In Europe, the fastback had been around for a long time. The mainstay of Porsche's production was the coupe. Aston Martin's DB2 was also mainly sold as a coupe. But the Italians, with their Ferraris, Lancias and Maseratis, were the innovators; they introduced the "berlinetta," which, more or less loosely translated, means "small coupe." The emergence of the Mercedes 300SL, in 1955, gave this closed body style a significant shot in the arm. First available only as a coupe, it was restyled as a roadster in 1957. Jaguar's E-type, introduced in 1961, came in both coupe and roadster versions.

So did the Sting Ray. The first year's figures show that sales were divided equally between the two; about ten thousand were made of each. The following year the trend had swung in favor of the convertible. This trend continued for the entire Sting Ray run; in 1967 there were almost twice as many convertibles sold, 8,500 and 14,500, respectively.

For the first year of the fourth generation, 1968, the roadster still outsold the coupe two to one. But the following year a dramatic turnabout took place; there were now 22,000 coupes made, as opposed to 16,500 convertibles.

Was the turnabout attributable to the looks of the coupe? Or was it a matter of domestication? Did the makeup of the Corvette buyer change slowly? Did it swing toward a concern for safety and comfort? By 1971 the coupe outsold the convertible two to one. By the end of the convertible era, in 1975, the coupe dominated totally, outselling the open car seven to one.

Marty Scholand was always ready for a Corvette. All it took was for an old high school buddy, a salesman at a Chevrolet dealership in Rochester, New York, to wave to him as he passed in his Dodge Charger. On the lot sat a brand-new, last year model 1968 convertible. Less a result of the friend's salesmanship than of Marty's ripe condition, the Charger was traded

(continued on overleaf)

ver the years, demand for convertibles has varied. After the introduction of the new bodystyle in 1968, sales of roadsters dropped steadily, until in 1975 GM called it quits. Less than five thousand were made that last year. Marty Scholand, East Berlin, Pennsylvania, owns this pristine Orange Flame copy, chassis number 1Z67J5S413884. In fact, with just over two thousand miles on the odometer, this decade-old Survivor is still brand new!

in. That was the beginning. After having owned a string of various Corvettes, he now has a well-rounded collection consisting of a 1953 (in need of restoration), a 1963 Sting Ray coupe (won Best of Show at the 1973 NCCC Convention in Indianapolis), the 1975 convertible (has gone just over 2,000 miles), and a 1978 Pace Car.

Marty is lucky to be able to own the cars he dreamed about as a boy, but even more lucky to be able to share his avocation with his wife, Connie. (In fact, she owns the 1975.) Together they are active in the local York County Corvette Club, counting close to 50 members. A now-legendary annual event, the Fourth of July Rally is hosted by Connie and Marty. They have also attended several events on the national level. Illustrating that Connie is not just a tagalong is the fact that she won the Ladies Class at the 1980 regional NCCC drag meet. Her time was 14.20. Marty also competed (although, not in the ladies event). They both drove the same machine, the Pace Car. Fortunately, for the preservation of peace and harmony in the family, Marty beat her time, but by only one tenth of a second.

Marty's (Connie's) convertible was originally delivered to a dealer in Philadelphia, who in turn was to present it to Bobby Clarke, Most Valuable Player of the NHL that year and a member of the Philadelphia Flyers hockey team. Due to a last-minute disagreement, the car instead went to a doctor in Dover, Delaware. He bought it for his wife, but she was not comfortable with the four-speed, so the car went on to Downington, Pennsylvania, where it was stored for over a year, until Marty got it in 1977.

The plane is taxiing toward the hangar, its motor revving, its propellor whizzing, its rudders flapping. We better move. Quickly. Marty tells me to drive, and as we make our getaway (Marty still in possession of the microfilm), accelerating down the narrow road, open fields surrounding us on both sides, the drowning sun coloring the horizon red, the cool wind pinching the skin, I am again reminded of the true spirit of the classic sports car.

What a shame that era had to end.

This collection of never-before-published photographs show some of the various stages the fourth-generation Corvette went through on its way to final product in 1968. A close-up study of each photograph would surely reveal a multitude of abandoned details and concepts, too complex to expand on here. But, touching on just a few in brief: opposite page, bottom, the row of three photos show a rear window similar to the one on the Sting Ray. Top, far right, shows a much more attractive rear end design, with the tails of the scoop longer and straighter. This page, closing in on the final look.

78

Commemorative Commodity.

In 1978 the Corvette had been around for 25 years. To the enthusiasts who had followed its growth from the first stumbling steps in 1953, through the gradual rise to eminence, both in the marketplace as well as on the racetrack, and to the engineers and designers and marketing men who had constructed and created and promoted, who had fought the battles to keep it alive, there was cause for celebration.

Looking at world events, the path leading through those 25 years was full of unforseen turmoil. The latter half alone had seen both the assassination as well as the impeachment of a US President, the abundance of energy as well as the apparent lack of it, war as well as its painful ending, recessions as well as periods of expansion. There had been the American bicentennial celebration. There had been the hippies. There had been the Beatles. And there had been the disco craze. The Corvette had survived it all.

In 1978 the biggest problem facing the auto industry was inflation. The annual rate was close to ten percent. It took $200 of 1978 money to buy the goods you paid $100 for in 1967. For example, the base price for a Corvette coupe was $4,388 in 1967; $9,351 in 1978.

Jimmy Carter was President. The Camp David Accord was signed. Muhammed Ali lost his crown, but won it back later in the year, becoming the first to twice recapture the title. The New York Yankees beat the Los Angeles Dodgers to win the World Series for the second time in a row. Bjorn Borg won at Wimbledon for the third time in a row. Woody Allen's *Annie Hall* got the Oscar for best film. Dolly Parton was named

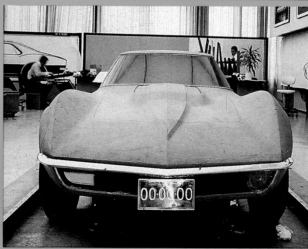

Pictured here is a variety of nose jobs. On this page, the two photographs above show what the designers came up with, trying to meet the impact regulations in 1973. The photograph to the left shows the stylists experimenting with the shape of the turn signals. On the opposite page, the finished products: top, the 1968 and 1969 nose. In 1970 the grille received the "egg-crate" grille and square turn signals. Center, the 1973 urethane bumper. In 1975, although reengineered beneath the skin, the only external difference was small rubber pads. Bottom, the 1980 redesign lasted to the end of the fourth generation.

entertainer of the year by the Country Music Association. And Mario Andretti became the second American to capture the World Championship title in Formula One.

In 1961 the auto industry had seen a low point of 5.4 million cars manufactured. In 1973 it had reached a high point, 9.9. Things were bad again in 1975; down to 6.4. In 1978 the figures were back up again, to 8.9. The sales of Corvettes, however, did not follow these trends. In 1961, production reached a new high; the 20,000 barrier was broken. In 1973 the 30,000 barrier met with the same destiny. In 1975 the sales figures nibbled at the 40,000 mark. And in 1978 total output came close to 50,000 units. The Corvette had shown remarkable progress and adaptability, thanks to the skill of the people whose job it was to sense the market. When styling gimmicks were in fashion, the Corvette got its share. When there was a cry for horsepower, the Corvette became even more muscular. When there was talk of smaller displacement and energy conservation, the Corvette met those demands as well.

The 1978 Indianapolis 500 was hot and fast, with 350,000 fans ensuring high temperatures in the bleachers, and a scorching sun guaranteeing a track reading of 120 degrees. Danny Ongais, in a Parnelli/Cosworth snatched the lead from pole-sitter Tom Sneva, driving a Penske/Cosworth. Ongais held on to the lead until lap 70, when Al Unser, also Cosworth powered in Jim Hall's Lola, managed to pass. The two dueled for much of the race, with Unser continuously in the lead. On lap 145 Ongais had to give up the chase due to a burned-out rotor on his turbocharger. On lap 179, with Sneva now 28 seconds behind in second place, Unser was held up when he overshot his pit and caused some damage to the car. This was the last pit stop, and when both contenders were back circling the track again, it was evident how close the race had become. During these last exciting laps Unser managed to hold on to the lead, finally crossing the finish line as the winner, eight seconds

(continued on overleaf)

New for 1978 was the fastback styling, reminiscent of the old Sting Ray. While reminiscing, GM decided to make something special to commemorate the 25th Anniversary of the Corvette. Featured here is the Limited Edition replica of the Indianapolis Pace Car. Just over six thousand were minted. California enthusiast Sy Baylos of La Palma, owns this beauty, chassis number 1Z87L8S904021.

ahead of Sneva. It was Unser's third win and the second closest ever.

This was the atmosphere in which Chevrolet had chosen to celebrate the 25th anniversary of their sports car; pacing these horsepower giants was a special Corvette, distinctively dressed up for the occasion.

The original plan called for a limited edition of 1,000 replicas of the Indianapolis Pace Car. Various color combinations were tested; black on the upper body and silver on the lower was the alternative finally settled on. In addition to the fastback styling, new for that year, the Pace Car also sported prominent front and rear spoilers. Completing the exterior dress-up was a set of decals for the doors and rear side panels. The application of these was left up to the owner. Most thought they were too much and left them in their wrappers. The interior also received special treatment; the seats featured a design similar to the ones to be introduced the following year. Silver was the only interior color, but there was a choice of all-leather or leather and vinyl combined. The sticker price of the Pace Car was 13,653 dollars. This included most of the available comfort options. The decision on engine and transmission was up to the customer.

As word of the limited edition spread, so did demand. Instead of only 1,000, it was decided to produce one for each dealer, or roughly 6,500 units. Demand had its way with the price as well. Many reportedly went for double the amount on the sticker.

The anniversary would have been the perfect occasion to introduce an all-new Corvette. But the Pace Car was not this long-overdue machine. It was not even representative of a high point in Corvette styling and performance. Nevertheless, it was the machine Corvette chose to bring out in commemoration of its anniversary. And, as such, it will always be special.

At the point of this writing, six years later, the Pace Car has lost some of its original sparkle and value. But, it will make a come back. Rest assured. All it takes is time.

In 1978 the Corvette celebrated its 25th anniversary. To mark the occasion the Limited Edition Indy Pace Car was issued. An exact replica of the pace car used in that year's Indianapolis 500, the limited edition immediately became a popular collectors item. The pictures above, show the Pace Car in full regalia. To the left, a photograph showing a prototype for testing the effect of various paint schemes. Opposite page, the search for new shapes never stops. Some ideas make it, others don't. This series of never-before-published photographs from the the GM files show some that didn't.

80

Encounter With Space Ship Corvette.

Like people and animals, cars, too, send signals. It has to do with looks. We do not expect a corpulent man to be quick and agile. But we do expect a deer to possess those qualities.

The sleekness of the E-type Jaguar made it look light and fast. The similarly styled D-type, however, even though it was faster, did not look as fast; it looked more powerful, thanks to its rounder, more massive body. One of the fastest sedans ever, the Mercedes 300SEL 6.3, certainly did not look like it could outrun, by two to one, Michelotti's sleek little Triumph Spitfire. The Mercedes, of course, was not intended to look fast; it had what it took without showing it. The Triumph, on the other hand, could afford only the look, not the goods.

These observations, subjective, and certainly kept on a most primitive level, do lead to a question: What kind of signals do the various Corvette models send?

The 1953, in spite of its toothy grin, did not look particularly fast or ferocious. The most effective speed-evoking element was the windshield. True, the body was low, but it was also too massive looking, somewhat pudgy. And there was a submissive look to those headlights, in the way they peered up at you.

The 1956 restyling improved matters a lot. The headlights now had a more purposeful expression. The downward motion of the rear made it look like it was ready to leap, like it had its hind legs firmly and capably planted on the ground.

Four basic tail end designs characterized the fourth-generation Corvette. Above, the original design stayed unchanged until 1974 when the new regulations forced the introduction of the urethane bumpers, opposite page, bottom. For 1974 it was a two-piece design, with a seam running vertically down the middle. In 1975 it was a one-piece design. Guards with a rubber pad had also been added. Above, a fastback window came in 1978. And in 1982, opposite page, top, it could finally be opened. There was also a spoiler, part of the bumper assembly rather than an add-on, as on the Pace Car.

Adding the cove to the side panel was a dramatic gesture; its presence certainly sent a signal of power and speed.

The 1958 addition of headlights and grilles did make the Corvette more mean looking, although not more beautiful, nor more refined.

The 1963 was a much more honest effort. Although it had certain dishonest features, such as fake vents, the basic styling relied purely on design. It sent out signals of power and speed in every direction. There were no headlights at all, no eyes, to communicate the message; their absence emphasized the purpose of the machine. The domes above the wheels, with their tapering tails, as well as the tapering tail of the fastback roof, all spelled speed. Where William Lyons was influenced by the sleek, ready-to-leap cat in his design of the XK120, William Mitchell took his inspiration from the smooth, flowing lines of a shark on the prowl.

While the 1963 Sting Ray was at home in the deep, the 1968 Stingray seemed to belong on the surface; there's one wave after another, and behind them, a vacuum, a wake, and a little spout from the propellor. Well, cars were not animals anymore; they began to look like paper planes, wedges, arrows. In 1970 Pininfarina finally sent the sports car into space with his Ferrari Modulo dream car.

These scattered thoughts come drizzling into my mind as I stand at the bottom of a gravel pit outside Pontiac, Michigan, shivering from the early morning chill, looking at Bob Larivee's 1980 Corvette. This is the closest a Corvette ever came to space! As I stand there the sun rises above the edge of the gravel mountain, sending long slices of light that greedily reach for the awesome looking, all-black machine, like the rays from the guns of the Martians I fully expect to show up next, silhouetted against the sky up there on the ridge. That's the sort of signals this Corvette sends. With its flat, massive, chromeless look, its spoiler fins, its nostrils, its curved glass surfaces, its mirrored roof panels, the Corvette

(continued on overleaf)

Martians are invading, and they are flying black Corvettes! Remarkably enough, after twelve years, the old body style could still excite. Of course, it had been updated from time to time. For 1980, the smoothly integrated spoilers did their thing, visually, and aerodynamically. The captured intruder chassis number 1Z878AS432749, belongs to Bob Larivee of Pontiac, Michigan.

looks like the amalgamation of a Star Wars monster and a Darth Vader helmet.

Bob Larivee is a car enthusiast whose sphere of interest is uncommonly broad; his collection consists of not only a 57 Chevy (original, low mileage), but also a Ferrari Lusso, a 31 Cadillac V-16 Dual Cowl Phaeton (People's Choice at Black Hawk and Third in Class at Pebble Beach), and a 32 Ford Phaeton hot rod, just to mention a few. But, confesses Bob, he is, above all, a Trans Am man; he has quite a variety of those. And, of course, he has a selection of Corvettes; there are at least four of them stored in various places. A Sting Ray (his favorite), an all-red 62, a 78 Pace Car with only 20 miles on the odometer, are some of them. The last two are on loan to Harrah's in Reno. The 1980 is the driver. He keeps it near at hand behind his office.

Bob was born in Detroit. His first significant involvement with cars occurred when he entered the Soap Box Derby. He was 15 then. At 21, he started racing real cars. That career lasted until 1977. In the beginning he raced Ford flatheads. Later he switched to Chevrolet power, racing both small-blocks as well as big-blocks, Chevys as well as Camaros.

Bob's business, Group Promotions, naturally revolves around cars. For more than a quarter of a century now, it has produced custom car shows all over the US and Canada. In fact, it is now the largest car show organization in the world, running a packed schedule, totaling approximately one hundred events per year.

The shooting is over. The sun is up. But the new day is still cold. Fortunately, I can start it off with a drive in Corvette's hot space ship. Lighter now than before, thanks to lower-density roof panels, reduced gauge in hood and doors, thinner glass, reduced gauge in the frame, and new aluminum differential housing as well as cross member, the signals sent by that awesome-looking body are not empty threats.

Oh yes, I discovered that the speedometer now stops at 85 mph. That's very convenient: You don't have to worry about the degree of bad conscience anymore!

During the seventies the Corvette continued to be a force to reckon with in racing. Lack of space allows only a limited sampling: Allan Barker, opposite page, top, was the SCCA B-Production Champion more than once. Corvettes did well in endurance events: Daytona, Sebring and Le Mans. To the right, Dave Heinz and Bob Johnson took fourth overall at Sebring in 1972, best ever for a Corvette. Far right, Jerry Hansen was the 1980 B-Production Champion. Here he is seen winning at Road Atlanta. This page, Le Mans in 1976; John Greenwood had one of the best times during practice but was not able to finish.

84

Dedicated to Design.

There is that seen-in-so-many-pictures court-yard, its floor covered with that dark-brown, hexagonal-shaped tile. It is completely secluded from the outside world, surrounded by a twice-man-size wall. Immediately inside that wall, a tight row of long-limbed, neatly trimmed trees form a second line of defense.

And there is that landmark dome, with its series of always-curtained, green-tinted windows running all around the base, and, above it, its silvery roof, arching to infinity.

This is the viewing complex at General Motors' Design Center in Warren, Michigan. It is holy ground. It is to the man involved with auto-motive design what the White House lawn is to the man following presidential politics. Since the mid-fifties, every design to emerge from GM, be it sports car, family sedan or utility van, have all had a meeting with destiny here.

Today, a sunny afternoon in the fall of 1983, the courtyard is occupied by a red Corvette. It is the personal car of its chief designer, Jerry Palmer. He and I, plus the man in charge of moving it, plus the man in charge of detailing it — this is union territory — stand around, admiring the slick, shining beauty.

"The Coke-bottle waist is gone. The exaggerated fender domes are gone. All the excesses are gone. But it's still a Corvette!" I say, my arm sweeping the length of the smooth body.

"Yes, that was one of the basic goals for the new design," Jerry says. He seems to be energized by a genuine enthusiasm.

The process of designing a new car is a long one, the path littered with spent ideas and efforts. By the end of 1979, the Corvette designers had arrived at the final shape. On the opposite page, top, the full-size clay mockup is getting a last touch-up before the paint-simulating coating is applied. Pictured to the right and far right, front ends featuring headlight designs that were later abandoned. Above and to the left, for the new Corvette, the designers didn't concern themselves just with the exterior: engine compartment, and especially induction housing, received a lot of attention.

"The new design had to carry on the Corvette heritage," he continues. "The design is really very straightforward. The surface development is based on what's underneath. And underneath is a machine. In other words, designers and engineers worked hand in hand. The main hurdle was the location of the engine. Once that was decided the project took off."

"You were involved in the mid-engine Aero-Vette project. What was behind the decision to go with the front-engine instead?"

"Well, first of all we had the Corvette tradition to consider. Then we had the introduction of Porsche's 928. If a manufacturer who had built its reputation on rear-engined cars now saw fit to go with the engine up front, then, certainly, we knew the climate was changing. But more than that, our own engineers were sure they could keep the front-engine position and still achieve ideal weight distribution.

"Another hurdle was passed when engineers and designers together came up with a solution that lowered the H-point of the car." Jerry goes on. "We created a larger central tunnel that made room for the exhaust system and allowed for an almost horizontal driveline. This was crucial. It meant that the base of the windshield could be lowered, which in turn enabled us to lower the entire car."

Jerry Palmer is a product of Detroit. Not only was he born in the automotive capital of the world — the year was 1942 — but he also received his education there. His father was a car salesman. What else? And young Jerry was already early-on sketching cars, in fact, anything connected with transportation, trains, boats, planes. In 1962 he enrolled in the Art School for the Society of Arts and Crafts. In 1964 he was accepted for a summer program at GM Styling. The following year he was hired full-time. His early involvements were with the boattail Buick Riviera and the Chevrolet Vega.

To have been so completely educated in the "School of Detroit" may seem like a handicap,

(continued on overleaf)

Worth the wait? Unequivocally, yes! A more worthy, a more fitting, a more valid replacement would be difficult to imagine. From its shape to its handling it displays the thoughtful thoroughness of its creators. It is in one stroke both advanced, and, something the Corvette often lacked, refined. In these photographs, the personal car of Corvette designer Jerry Palmer, chassis number 1G1AY0782E5118028, is captured at its birthplace, General Motors Technical Center in Warren, Michigan.

maybe not from the viewpoint of learning how to work within the system, but from the viewpoint of individual growth. However, Jerry's accomplishments — his design group was responsible for the 1982 Camaro as well — certainly do not support these fears. When confronted with the question, Jerry credits the special freedom that exists at GM Design. All the chiefs, Harley Earl, Bill Mitchell, and presently Irv Rybicki — with Chuck Jordan immediately responsible for the Corvette project — have always given their designers freedom to explore and experiment.

In 1972 Jerry, Chuck Jordan and Henry Haga, were involved in the Aero-Vette program. In 1974, when Haga left for Opel, Jerry took over as chief of Chevrolet Exterior 3.

The 1984 Corvette is Jerry's eighth. He also owns a Ferrari 308 GTB. From a styling viewpoint, some of his favorites are Ferrari's 330P4 and 512S, Porsche's 917 and the Lola T70.

"So, how do you feel about it now, seeing it all finished?" I ask Jerry.

"Well, one of the things we wanted was a wheel-oriented look. We accomplished that. We also wanted to shorten the distance between front axle and dash. We accomplished that, too. In fact, looking at it now, it came out remarkably close to one of the first sketches I made back in 1976!" Jerry says.

It is time to take pictures. The man in charge of moving the Corvette is set in motion: the angle of the car in relation to the dome must be just right. A lot of back-and-forth adjusting follows. Then the services of the man in charge of detailing is called upon: the tires are a little too shiny.

Everything looks all right now. I have the car and its creator framed in the camera. I ask him to say something, anything, just to give his face expression. He could have said cheese. Instead, subconsciously, his mind comes up with another word, a word that embodies the relentless search for the perfect shape in every little detail, the sum of which is the new Corvette. He says it with that energized enthusiasm.

"This car is designed... designed... designed..."

The fourth-generation Corvette lasted an unprecedented fifteen seasons. During all those years the designers had, of course, been working on various ideas for a replacement. Most efforts revolved around a mid-engine concept. The first fairly firm ideas for the new front-engine Corvette took shape in 1976. Chief designer Jerry Palmer's sketch from that year shows how close the final product came to the initial concept. The first full-scale mockup was completed in 1978. The series of photographs on these pages show some of the intermediate steps that led to the final shape.

The Survivors Series

By Henry Rasmussen

"Corvettes for the Road," ninth in The Survivors Series, was photographed, designed and written by Henry Rasmussen. Assistant designer was Walt Woesner. Copy editor, Barbara Harold. Tintype Graphic Arts of San Luis Obispo, California, supplied the typesetting. The color separations, as well as the printing and binding, were produced by South China Printing Company in Hong Kong. Liaison with the printer was Peter Lawrence.

The black and white pictures were mainly obtained from two sources: the photo archives of General Motors Design, where Charles Jordan cleared the way, and Dominic Villari and Floyd Joliet helped with the research; and the library at Road & Track, under direction of Otis Meyer.

Special acknowledgements go to Chip Miller of York, Pennsylvania, for sharing both his wealth of knowledge as well as his connections in the Corvette world; to Bill Kosfeld of Motorbooks International for his pleasant handling of day-to-day matters connected with publishing; to Tom Warth, of Motorbooks International, whose continued support made yet another title in this series possible.

The author also wishes to thank these contributors: Deryl Cherry, William Clark, Art Fisher, Thomas Kreid, Raymond Pannone, Billy Sawyer, and Paul Sawyer.